Armchair Puzzlers™

Optical Teasers

Sink Back and Solve Away!™

Al Sec...

UNIVERSITY GAMES

Armchair Puzzlers™
Optical Teasers
Sink Back and Solve Away!®

Editorial Director: Erin Conley
Designers: Jeanette Miller, Lisa Yordy
Special thanks to Suzanne Cracraft, Lynn Gustafson, Audrey Haworth,
Emily Jocson, Jennifer Ko, Cris Lehman, Maria Llull, Bob Moog,
Tami Sartor and Nancy Spector for their invaluable assistance!

Printed in China.

ISBN 1-57528-955-5

CONTENTS

Introduction 5

Kitaoka's Waves...........................7

Revolving Circles Illusion 8

The Hermann Grid Illusion 9

The Ouchi Illusion......................10

Twisted Circles 11

An Illusion of Extent 12

A Surprised Policeman 13

School of Fish 14

Simultaneous Contrast Illusion 15

Shepard's Tabletop Illusion..........16

All the World's a Stage 17

The Café Escher Illusion..............18

Pinna's Deforming
Square Illusion 19

My Wife and Mother-in-Law 20

Wundt Illusion...........................21

The Impossible Fork 22

The Missing Clown ...., ...23

Kitchen Utensils 24

The Captain Has
Abandoned Ship 25

Does He Speak the Truth? 26

The Scintillating Grid Illusion 27

Day's Sine Wave Illusion 28

Can a Frog Turn into a Horse? 29

Estimation Illusion.....................30

Legs of Two Different Genders 31

Kitaoka's Spa Illusion 32

Morellet's Tiret Illusion 33

Assimilation Illusion 34

The Impossible Shelf 35

The Hering Illusion 36

Terra Subterranea 37

The Mysterious Lips 38

Where is the Dog's Master?..........39

Reflect on This 40

Coming and Going 41

Misaligned Eyes 42

Mochi ...., ...43

Let Sleeping Dogs Lie.................44

Figure/Ground Illusion #1 45

Adelson's Checker-Shadow
Illusion 46

The Glowing Lightbulb 47

Where is the Queen? 48

Kissing Couple 49

Rubin's Face/Vase Illusion 50

Splitting Lines Illusion 51
The Hula Hoop Illusion 52
Reversible Cube 53
A Dog's Life 54
Helen Keller 55
Egyptian Tête-à-tête 56
Figure/Ground Illusion #2 57
Todorovic's Dartboard Illusion 58
Muller-Lyer Illusion 59
The Twisted Cord Illusion 60
Upside Down 61
L'Egistential Quandry 62
Reflections on the
Word Mirror 63
Tilt Induction Illusion 64
Ehrenstein Illusion 65
Fisheye Illusion 66
Kitaoka's Kozoll 67
Cat and Mouse..........................68
The Ponzo Illusion 69
Time Saving Suggestion..............70
Illusory Spots and Circles 71
A Boy Grows a Beard 72
Pinna's Intertwining Illusion 73

Eye am a Mouth.........................74
Backwards Glance 75
Diamond Brightness Illusion........76
Sailing Through the
Palm Trees 77
An Artist's View of Reality...........78
Two Bodies are Better
Than One.................................79
Rising Lines 80
Sara Nader 81
The Hallway Illusion...................82
Bent Circles..............................83
A Glowing Portrait 84
Wade's Spiral............................85
Distorted Square Illusion 86
A Speed Reading Test.................87
A Sense of Foreboding................88
Glee Turns Glum.......................89
Jastrow's Duck/Rabbit Illusion.....90
What's This?..............................91
Impossible Figures 92
An Impossible Staircase..............93
The End is in Sight 94

4

INTRODUCTION

Welcome to the world of illusions. Prepare yourself to be tricked, fooled, bamboozled and perplexed, and there is NOTHING you can do about it!

However, it is important to understand that the eye puzzlers in this amazing collection are NOT an intelligence test. It does not matter how smart you are, how cultured you are, how experienced you are, or how old you are—anyone with normal vision will be fooled.

You will encounter static images that move, glow and flash. Size and shape will lose their meaning. You will be amazed at how things will change when you turn them upside down or shake them. Sometimes you will find it very hard to believe the captions and answers, and even then you may still not believe it!

When you go through the many illusions in this book, ask yourself the following questions: "Why am I being tricked in this way?" "Why am I not seeing what is really there?" These are fundamental questions about the workings of your own inner mind, parts of which you have little control over. You are fooled by the illusions in this book for the very same reasons you see the world accurately most of the time. Your brain interprets what it sees.

Your brain uses a set of rules to interpret and make sense of the very complex world in which you move about. These rules are very good at interpreting your world but sometimes these rules can also lead to mistakes, and these mistakes are called illusions. Luckily, your perceptual system has many methods for correcting such mistakes, so you rarely see illusions in the real world.

Even though illusions are rare in nature, they can be created. Interestingly, both artists and scientists have discovered many of the illusions in this book. Artists have discovered illusions as they sought to find new ways to represent painted scenes more realistically, and scientists have discovered illusions while trying to probe the inner workings of the visual/perceptual system.

6

Illusions are also fun and surprising, and I hope the examples in this book will provide you with some insight into the workings of your own inner mind. Now, go have some fun!

—Al Seckel

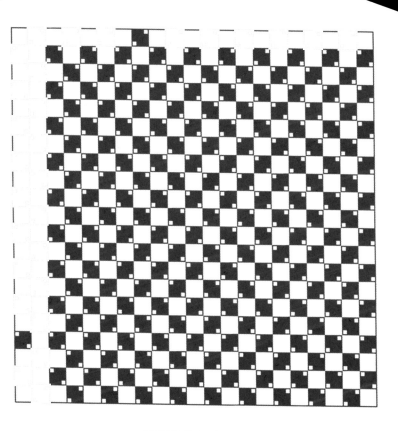

KITAOKA'S WAVES
Do the lines appear to be wavy?

Answer: They are all perfectly straight.

THE REVOLVING CIRCLES ILLUSION
Move your head slowly toward and away from the image and you will see
something very strange! The circles will turn in different ways.

THE HERMANN GRID ILLUSION

Count the faint dark dots at the intersections. When you are done, try counting again. If you stare at any one dot, it will disappear.

9

THE OUCHI ILLUSION
Slowly shake this image. The center section will appear to separate from the rest of the image.

10

TWISTED CIRCLES

Do you see a series of warped circles? Try tracing the lines. Be careful!
It is really a series of circles, each one within a larger circle.

11

12

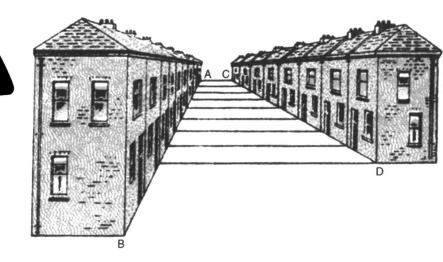

AN ILLUSION OF EXTENT
Which line is longer: Line A-B or Line C-D?

Answer: They are both the same length.

A SURPRISED POLICEMAN
This policeman will look really surprised when you
turn him upside down.

13

SCHOOL OF FISH
Are the fish swimming to the right or to the left?

Answer: Both! If you stare at the image, they will appear to reverse direction.

15

SIMULTANEOUS CONTRAST ILLUSION

Does the horizontal bar appear lighter on the left and darker on the right?
Try covering everything surrounding the bar to check your answer.

Answer: The bar is the same color on both sides.

SHEPARD'S TABLETOP ILLUSION
Which tabletop appears larger? Carefully measure them to check your answer.

Answer: They are both equal.

ALL THE WORLD'S A STAGE
Two musicians gather together to form the face of the famous 16th century
English playwright William Shakespeare.

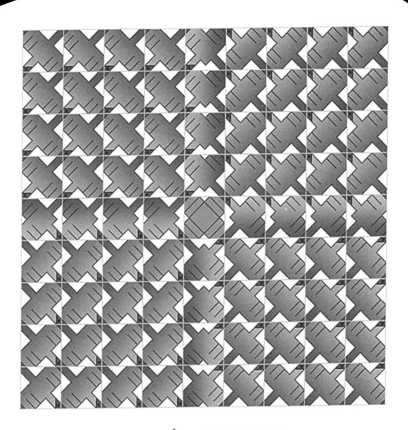

THE CAFÉ ESCHER ILLUSION
Do the horizontal and vertical lines bend? Check them with a straight edge.

Answer: The lines are perfectly straight.

19

PINNA'S DEFORMING SQUARE ILLUSION
Try slowly shaking and turning this image. The squares will appear to change shape and wiggle.

MY WIFE AND MOTHER-IN-LAW

Try to find both an old and young woman.

Answer: The eye of the old woman becomes the ear of the young woman. The mouth of the old woman becomes a necklace on the young woman.

20

THE WUNDT ILLUSION

E appears larger than D, which appears larger than C, which appears larger than B, which appears larger than A. So, which is the largest shape?

Answer: They are all equal in size and shape.

THE IMPOSSIBLE FORK
Do you see two rectangular prongs or three cylindrical prongs?

23

THE MISSING CLOWN
The circus seems to have lost its clown. Try to find him.

Answer: Turn the image 90° counterclockwise to see the clown.

24

KITCHEN UTENSILS
How many kitchen utensils can you find?

Answer: Don't forget to count both the black and white kitchen utensils.

25

THE CAPTAIN HAS ABANDONED SHIP
During the storm, the ship seems to have lost its captain. Try to find him.

Answer: Turn the image 90° clockwise to find him.

26

DOES HE SPEAK THE TRUTH?
Is this man telling the truth? The answer is written in his face.

Answer: He is a liar. Turn the image 90° counterclockwise to see why.

THE SCINTILLATING GRID ILLUSION

Count the faint dark dots at the intersections. When you are done,
try counting again. If you stare at any one dot, it will disappear.

28

DAY'S SINE WAVE ILLUSION
Are some vertical lines longer than others in this wave pattern?

Answer: They are all of equal length.

29

CAN A FROG TURN INTO A HORSE?
This strange frog won't turn into a prince. But it will turn into a horse!
Can you figure out how?

Answer: Turn the image 90° counterclockwise to find the horse.

ESTIMATION ILLUSION
How far up the triangle is the dot?

Answer: It is exactly in the middle.

30

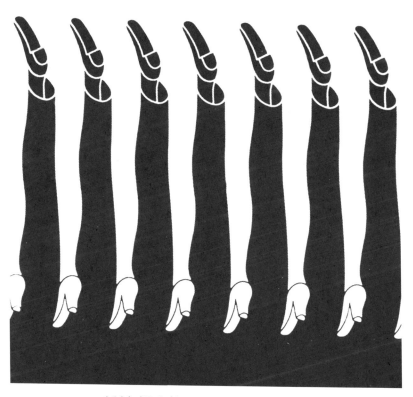

LEGS OF TWO DIFFERENT GENDERS
Can you see both the women's and men's legs?

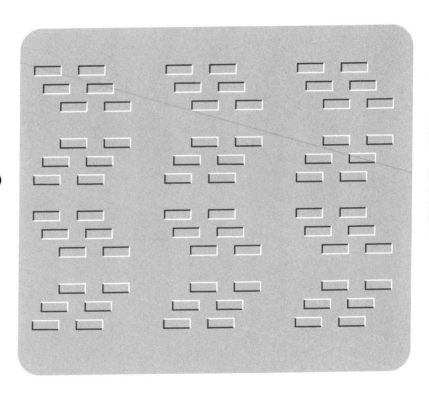

KITAOKA'S SPA ILLUSION
Move the image up and down slowly, and you will see the little shapes moving in strange ways.

MORELLET'S TIRET ILLUSION
Move your eyes around the edge of this image and it will appear to flash.

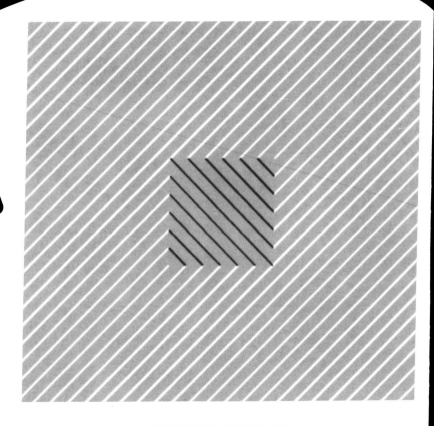

34

ASSIMILATION ILLUSION
Does the gray square in the middle appear darker than the surrounding gray?

Answer: They are equal shades of gray.

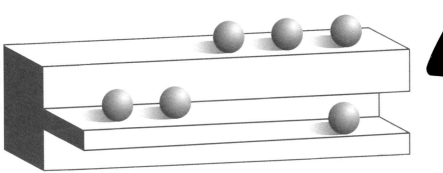

THE IMPOSSIBLE SHELF
What is wrong with this shelf?

36

THE HERING ILLUSION
Do the long lines bend?

Answer : They are all straight.

TERRA SUBTERRANEA

Does the monster in the background appear to be larger than the monster in the front? Try measuring each figure to test your answer.

Answer: They are equal in size.

THE MYSTERIOUS LIPS
Can you find the woman's face?

Answer: The houses are the eyes.

39

WHERE IS THE DOG'S MASTER?
This dog has lost its master. Try to find him.

Answer: Turn the image 90° clockwise to find him. The dog's ear becomes the man's hat.

REFLECT ON THIS

These numbers do not seem to add up correctly. Is there any way that you can make them add up correctly? You may have to reflect on this one a while.

Answer: Look at this image in a mirror.

COMING AND GOING
How can you make the ducks change direction?

Answer: Cover either the left or right outermost head.

42

MISALIGNED EYES
Does this man have crooked eyes? Check them with a straight edge.

Answer: His eyes are perfectly aligned.

MOCHI
Are the squares bent?

Answer: All the squares have straight edges.

43

44

LET SLEEPING DOGS LIE
**People on this island have an expression: "Let sleeping dogs lie."
Why do you think that is?**

Answer: The island is two sleeping dogs.

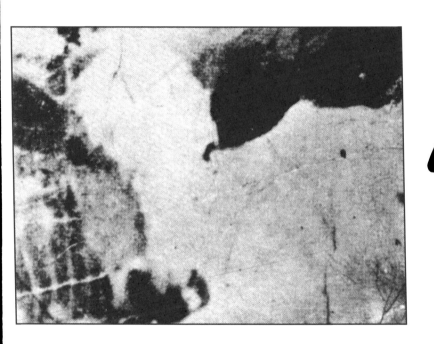

FIGURE/GROUND ILLUSION #1
What does this image represent?

Answer: The head of a cow.

45

ADELSON'S CHECKER-SHADOW ILLUSION

Are the light squares within the shadow the same shade of gray as the dark squares outside the shadow? Look through a small peephole to check

Answer: They are the same shade of gray.

THE GLOWING LIGHTBULB
Stare at this lightbulb for 30 seconds or more without averting your gaze. Quickly look at a blank sheet of paper and you will see a glowing lightbulb.

48

REX WHISTLER

WHERE IS THE QUEEN?

The king appears to have lost his queen.
Find her and put your finger on her hair.

Answer: Turn the king upside down.

KISSING COUPLE
Do you see one head or two heads kissing?

49

50

RUBIN'S FACE/VASE ILLUSION
Can you find the two profiles?

Answer: They are on either side of the vase.

SPLITTING LINES ILLUSION
Slowly move the image up and down and the lines will split.

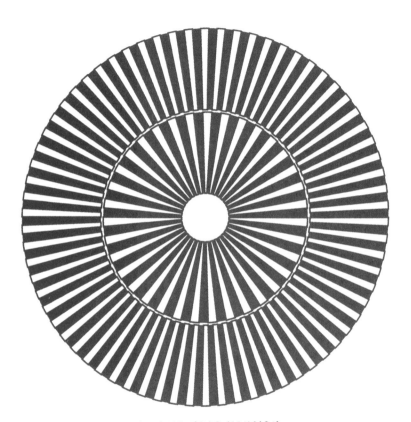

THE HULA HOOP ILLUSION
Slowly move this image in a circular fashion, like you are swirling water in a cup.

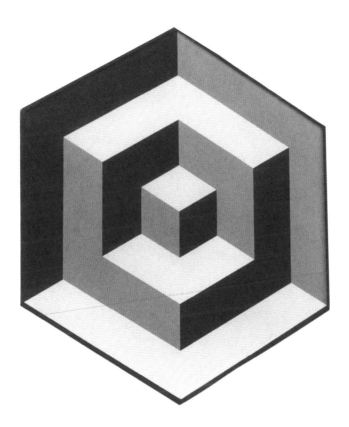

REVERSIBLE CUBE

If you stare at this image long enough, it will reverse. The insides of the cubes will become the outsides of the cubes.

A DOG'S LIFE
Does this dog think it is human?

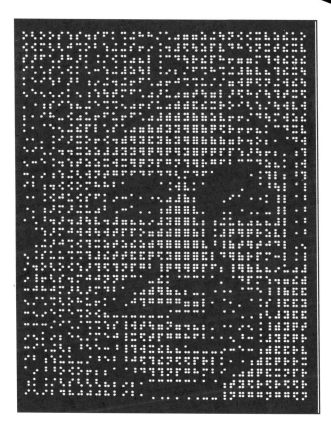

HELEN KELLER
This portrait of Helen Keller, who was blind since birth, is made
entirely out of Braille.

EGYPTIAN TÊTE-À-TÊTE
Do you see one face or two faces?

Answer: There is one face behind the candlestick and two on each side of the candlestick.

FIGURE/GROUND ILLUSION #2
What does this image represent?

Answer: A Dalmatian dog.

57

58

TODOROVIC'S DARTBOARD ILLUSION
Is the light area at Position 1 lighter than the dark area at Position 2?

Answer: Believe it or not, they are identical.

MULLER-LYER ILLUSION
Which horizontal length between the arrows is longer?
Does the ruler help?

Answer: The lengths are equal.

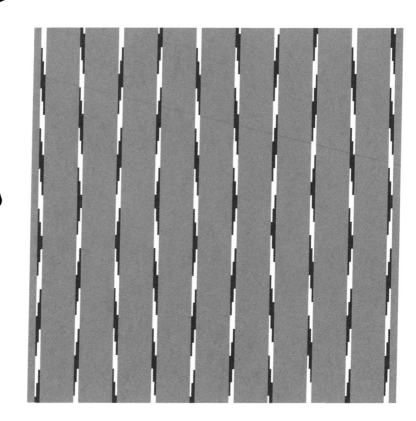

THE TWISTED CORD ILLUSION
Do the vertical lines bend?

Answer: They are perfectly straight.

UPSIDE DOWN
What does this say when you turn it upside down?

61

62

L'EGISTENTIAL QUANDRY
Why might this elephant have some difficulty walking?

REFLECTIONS ON THE WORD MIRROR
You can read the word mirror front to back.

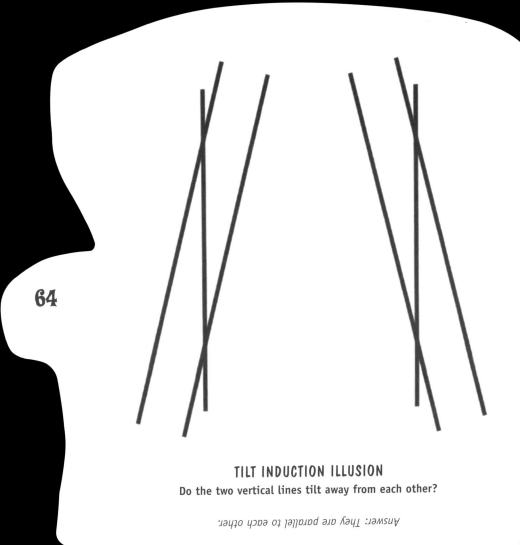

64

TILT INDUCTION ILLUSION
Do the two vertical lines tilt away from each other?

Answer: They are parallel to each other.

EHRENSTEIN ILLUSION

Do you see circles, even though there are no edges to make them? Do they appear to be brighter than their surroundings?

Answer: The circles are illusory and so is their brightness.

FISHEYE ILLUSION
Move this image close to your eye. It will no longer appear distorted.

66

KITAOKA'S KOZOLL
Do the horizontal lines tilt with respect to each other?

Answer: They are all parallel to each other.

A MOUSE HIDING FROM A CAT
This mouse is pretty clever!
Can you find where it is hiding from the cat?

THE PONZO ILLUSION
Is the bar on the left smaller than the bar on the right?

Answer: They are equal in size.

70

TIME-SAVING SUGGESTION
Try to see both the running figures and the arrows.

ILLUSORY SPOTS AND CIRCLES
Do you see a series of concentric rings made of little dots?

Answer: Both the dots and the rings are illusory.

A BOY GROWS A BEARD
Can you help this boy turn into a man?

Answer: Turn him upside down and he will grow a beard.

PINNA'S INTERTWINING ILLUSION
Do these rings appear to cross over each other?

Answer: They do not cross over each other. They are concentric circles.

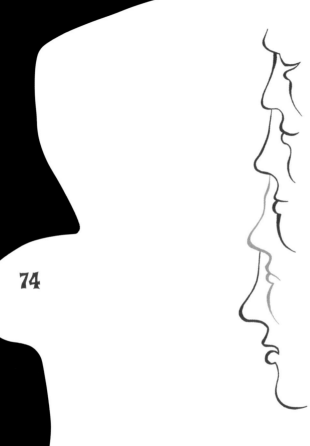

EYE AM A MOUTH
The eyes become the mouths.

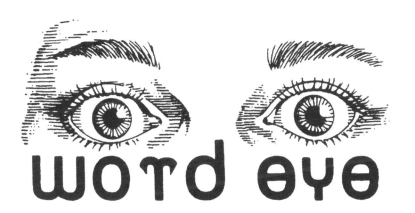

BACKWARDS GLANCE
What does this say when you read it in a mirror?

Answer: Eyebrow

DIAMOND BRIGHTNESS ILLUSION
Does the row of triangles on the bottom appear darker than the row at the top?

Answer: They are identical shades of gray.

SAILING THROUGH THE PALM TREES
Try to see both the palm trees and the boats.

AN ARTIST'S VIEW OF REALITY
What is strange about this painting?

TWO BODIES ARE BETTER THAN ONE
In this unretouched photograph, does the head belong to the lady on
the left or on the right?

Answer: Left

80

RISING LINES
Hold the page at eye level and look across it from the bottom right corner.
The lines will appear to rise from the page.

SARA NADER
Can you see the woman the musician is serenading?

THE HALLWAY ILLUSION
Does the man on the far right seem tiny compared with the man in the background? Measure them.

Answer: They are the same size.

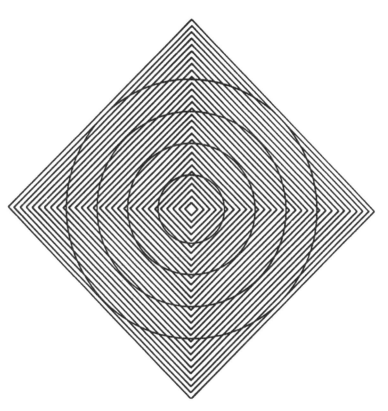

BENT CIRCLES
Do the circles bend?

Answer: They are perfectly round.

A GLOWING PORTRAIT
Stare at this image for at least 30 seconds without moving your eyes and then quickly look at a blank sheet of paper. You will see the woman appear to glow.

WADE'S SPIRAL
Do you perceive a spiral? Carefully trace it with your finger.

Answer: It is a series of concentric circles.

DISTORTED SQUARE ILLUSION
Does the left side of the square appear shorter than the right side?

Answer: They are the same length.

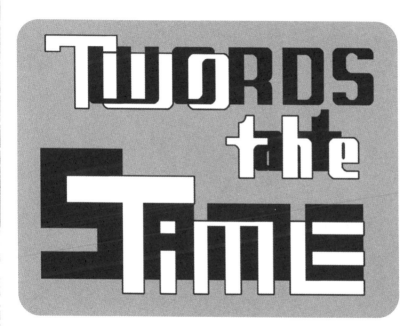

A SPEED READING TEST
Read all the words simultaneously. What do they say?

Answer: Two words at the same time.

88

A SENSE OF FOREBODING
Is there danger lurking for this couple?

Answer: There is a skull in the background.

GLEE TURNS GLUM
You can change the mood of these faces by turning them upside down.

JASTROW'S DUCK/RABBIT ILLUSION
Try to find both the duck and the rabbit.

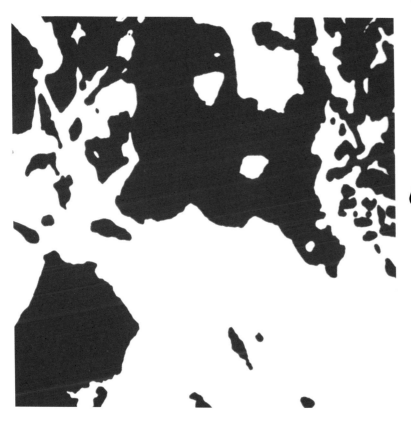

WHAT'S THIS?
What does this image represent?

Answer: A bearded man

IMPOSSIBLE FIGURES
Examine all of these figures. What is strange about them?

Answer: They are all impossible.

AN IMPOSSIBLE STAIRCASE
Can you locate the highest or lowest step?

Answer: There isn't one. That is why it is an impossible staircase.

94

the end

THE END IS IN SIGHT
Why was this illusion placed at the very end?
Turn it upside down to find out.

Answer: The End

9

Recommended Reading

If you are interested in learning more about illusions and why they work,
we recommend the following titles:

Al Seckel, *The Great Book of Optical Illusions*, Firefly Books, 2002

Al Seckel, *Incredible Visual Illusions: You Won't Believe Your Eyes,* Arcturus Publishing, 2003

Al Seckel, *Masters of Deception: Escher, Dali and Other Optical Illusion Artists*, Sterling, 2004

ABOUT THE AUTHOR

Al Seckel is the world's leading expert on visual and other types of sensory illusions. He has published several award-winning books on the science of illusions and lectures on this topic at many of the world's most prestigious universities. He is also active in building interactive galleries on illusions and perception for science museums around the world.

You can find out more about
Al Seckel at his web site: http://neuro.caltech.edu/~seckel

5